# CHRISTM
# SCISSOR SKILLS

## Activity Workbook For Preschool

Copyright © 2020

All rights reserved to Winter Creativity Publishing

No parts of this publication my be reproduced, distributed or transmitted in any form, or by any means, without prior written permission from the publisher

# This Book Belongs to:

Thank you for your purchase!
If you liked this book, we would truly appreciate a short review on our amazon product page. Reviews are very important for authors as it helps us understand your opinion, and therefore create more books that satisfy your needs.

# Color, Cut, and Paste inside the right box

# Color, Cut , and Paste inside the right box

# Color, Cut , and Paste inside the right box

# Color, Cut, and Paste inside the right box

# Color, Cut, and Paste inside the right box

# Color, Cut, and Paste inside the right box

# Color, Cut, and Paste inside the right box

# Color, Cut , and Paste inside the right box

# Color, Cut , and Paste inside the right box

# Color, Cut, and Paste inside the right box

# Christmas Counting
## Color, Cut and Paste the right number

# Christmas Counting
## Color, Cut and Paste the right number

# Christmas Counting
## Color, Cut and Paste the right number

# Christmas Counting
## Color, Cut and Paste the right number

# Christmas Counting
## Color, Cut and Paste the right number

# Christmas Counting
## Color, Cut and Paste the right number

# Christmas Guessing
## What picture comes next?

# Christmas Guessing
## What picture comes next?

# Christmas Guessing
## What picture comes next?

# Christmas Guessing
## What picture comes next?

# Christmas Coloring
# Color and Cut the illustration

# Christmas Coloring
# Color and Cut the illustration

# Christmas Coloring
# Color and Cut the illustration

# Christmas Coloring
## Color and Cut the illustration

# Christmas Coloring
# Color and Cut the illustration

# Christmas Coloring
# Color and Cut the illustration

# Christmas Coloring
# Color and Cut the illustration

# Christmas Coloring
## Color and Cut the illustration

Made in the USA
Columbia, SC
03 November 2023